MW01107492

God Can Use You, Too!

God Can Use You, Too!

By

A. X. Hailey

Editor
Ray Glandon

Senior Publisher
Steven Lawrence Hill Sr.

Awarded Publishing House
ASA Publishing Company
Established Since 2005

A Publisher Trademark Cover page

ASA Publishing Company
Awarded Best Publisher for Quality Books 2008, 2009
105 E. Front St., Suite 201A, Monroe, Michigan 48161
www.asapublishingcompany.com

Copyrights©2012 A. X. Hailey, All Rights Reserved
Book: God Can Use You, Too!
Date Published: 07.01.12
Edition: 1 *Trade Paperback*
Book ASAPCID: 2380603
ISBN: 978-1-886528-38-3
Library of Congress Cataloging-in-Publication Data

This book was published in the United States of America.
State of Michigan

A Publisher Trademark Title page

Table of Contents

God Can Use You, Too!

Foreword

The relationship I share with Aloysius Xavier Hailey was forged during a period of both of our lives when we were teenagers transitioning into becoming young men. Now, some twenty years later, he, a licensed ordained minister, has spiritually developed into a mighty vessel used by GOD. Therefore, in this book, *God can use you, too*, the author allows the reader sacred access to encounter the experiences that have shaped the author into an instrument of GOD.

The author has always had an uncanny and unique ability to communicate with people. I have personally witnessed this because for several years the author and I were college roommates. During this period, I really began to appreciate the man that GOD was creating as Aloysius X. Hailey. He has a very straight forward and engaging way to help you see what you have always seen, but now, in a way you have never seen it. Through the years we have stayed in contact, and we have ended up doing the same thing: being used as ministers of God's great gospel!

As already mentioned, the author and I were college roommates. Both of us were very adept at finding our way into numerous sticky situations. In one situation, Aloysius's personality and charm was possibly the only thing that could have salvaged me from personal disaster. I remember I was being tortured, held hostage, and black-mailed by a young lady for whom I had a particular affection. I was in the college cafeteria (this was an embarrassing public spectacle). The young lady had a personal item that belonged to me, and I desperately needed it back. I had reached the point of despair to where I had sacrificed all pride and dignity. I was groveling. In fact, I was begging for mercy for the young lady to return the item. There was no way that I could communicate or articulate the dire straits of my situation. The young lady, clearly enjoying the control and power she had over my desperate state, would not return my personal effects. Just then, my roommate, the author, entered the cafeteria (if I remember correctly from baseball practice). He quickly assessed the situation and sensed my sincere desperation. Aloysius, with a unique charm, approached the young lady, and she willingly surrendered my personal belongings! In an instant the author was able to communicate what I could not, and, in a manner that I was unable! It is with similar gifts of charm, communication, and persuasion that the author brings to help you understand that God can use you, too!

In this book there is a format and a fashion that is certain to hold your attention. How so? The author has formatted each chapter to provide multiple perspectives surrounding each central thought. The language of this text is fashioned to relate to contemporary culture to eliminate the need of youth and young adults guessing or trying to figure out exactly what God wants you to know. The format allows you to see yourselves in the mirror as GOD sees you! You realize that you may not be as you have imagined. There is good and bad to the sights that the author will put before your eyes. The good is that you are worth more to God than you could ever imagine. The bad is that we may see ourselves far from completion. Furthermore, and most importantly, the good is that God not only can use you, too, but God also wants to use you NOW! That is exactly what this book will do! It will show you your worth and then show you how to work!

In reading this work, I encourage you to listen to the numerous voices and opinions that are scattered throughout the pages. This is a plea to personalize and prioritize your life with God. You will not only find the author's wisdom within these pages, but you will also find the wisdom of others, many of whom I personally know and respect. Therefore, as you read this book, it is not just the author's opinion that God can use you, there is a symphony of saints and a body of believers in Jesus Christ who believe that God not only "can" but "will" use your life to dynamically divulge His Glory. The question is not so much, can God use you, but will you allow Him to! I personally encourage you. JUST GIVE IN! Allow yourself to be blessed by GOD!

It is my prayer that this book blesses you in every way that you have intended by picking it up. Above and beyond this, may this book bless you in ways that only GOD can imagine (Ephesians 3:20).

Yours in the love of Christ,
Rev. Frederick D. James, Ph.D

Introduction

"...where the Spirit of the Lord is, there is freedom."
2Corinthians 3:17

My dear brothers and sisters, I greet you in the name of our Lord and Savior Jesus Christ. It is with great appreciation that I attempt to enlighten everyone on young people's importance to the Kingdom of God. I appreciate the fact that someone has taken the interest in choosing this book to read. I believe the Lord has placed in my spirit the desire and ability to write this book. It seems as if the young people in the Kingdom are often an overlooked entity. I've talked to a lot of young people, and many have expressed that church just isn't for them. Many of them go to church because their parent(s) make them go, and when they get there, they feel like sermons and bible lessons are not for them. In their minds, they don't feel like they're high priority because little emphasis is placed on them and their spiritual needs.

This book is not solely about going to church; it is about helping young people discover and understand their worth in God's Kingdom. God wants to use whomever is willing and available. The question is, when?

When will someone, anyone going to let God use them? Is it when they have gone out and done unsavory things? Is it when they go out and "sow one's wild oats?" Or is it when they have finished living the way they want?

My message to the reader of this book is that God wants to use them in the condition, size, age, race, socioeconomic, maturity, and intelligent state they're in. Let the Lord speak to you while reading. Ask Him to open your mind and spirit to receive what He has to say to you. I implore you to read! Read to get an understanding. Read, read, and read! We have too many young people who do not read. This book was written with that in mind. There is verbiage and vernacular that young people will recognize. However, there are also words that you may need a dictionary to understand. That was done to challenge and to broaden your thinking. So, I encourage you to not let the devil fool you into thinking that you are not worth anything. God has a plan for you and your life. Allow Him to use you as He pleases. God bless you, and I hope this book will be an inspiration to you.

"When I look back, I am so impressed again with the life-giving power of literature. If I were a young person today, trying to gain a sense of myself in the world, I would do that again by reading, just as I did when I was young."

-Maya Angelou

About The Author

Aloysius Xavier Hailey is from Detroit, MI. He serves as Associate Minister at Synagogue Baptist Church in Detroit under the leadership of Reverend Jake Gaines, Jr. It is there that he works on many different ministries including the youth department. He is a staff member of WMCK-Parker Bible Seminary as an Instructor and Logistical Coordinator. Minister Hailey received his Bachelor of Arts degree in Sociology from Paine College in Augusta, GA and played on their baseball team for four years. He also was a part of the school's Concert Choir, Arts Ensemble, and pledged Kappa Alpha Psi Fraternity, Inc. After graduation, Minister Hailey taught in the charter school system in Detroit for 13 years. He has also worked with youth in other capacities. He was a summer camp counselor for Camp Burt Shurly through the Detroit Public Schools, and he has worked for a non-profit organization (Abundant Care Training Services) teaching youth sports skills and life skills. Lastly, Minister Hailey is married to his college sweetheart, Sharon, and from this union has been blessed with two beautiful daughters, Ashur and Azariah.

Special Thanks

First and foremost, I would like to thank my Heavenly Father for using me to write these words and hopefully be an inspiration to someone that has decided to read this book. He has given me the avenue to express myself, and for that, I am deeply humbled. I would like to thank my wife, Sharon, for standing beside me throughout my writing of this book. She has been my inspiration and motivation for continuing to improve my knowledge. She is my rock, and I dedicate this book to her. I also thank my wonderful children: Ashur and Azariah, for always making me smile and for understanding that their daddy was working on something big. I hope that one day they can read this book and understand why I spent so much time in front of my computer. I'd like to thank my parents, grandparents, siblings, aunts, uncles, cousins, and friends for allowing me to follow my ambitions throughout my life. My families, including my in-laws, have always supported me, and I really appreciate it. I look forward to discussing this book with my family at future gatherings as I'm sure they will all read it soon.

Many thanks to my church families, in particular Synagogue Baptist Church and my pastor Rev. Jake Gaines Jr., who showed me the ropes in not only ministry, but in writing as well. Without that knowledge and encouragement, I wouldn't have ventured into writing this book. He has been in my corner from the very beginning. I thank the Lord for Pastor Jake Gaines, Jr., and the Synagogue family! Also, to Pastor Jesse L. Barber and the Williams Memorial church family who nurtured and watched me grow up from a boy to a man. You gave me my start and my foundation. You will never be forgotten.

I would like to thank the editor, Ray Glandon. He is so good at what he does that it's just ridiculous! He chopped up what I wrote after I thought I chopped it up enough! To the publishing company, ASA Publishing, thank you for taking a chance on somebody like me, a first time author. Thanks for everything; I look forward to writing the second book soon.

I also wish to thank all of the contributors to this book: co-laborer of the gospel, college roommate and one of my "besties," Reverend Dr. Frederick James; college friend and fraternity brother, Frankie Brown, college friend, Candance Greene; college friend and co-laborer Pastor Dominique Johnson; friend, brother, and co-laborer Reverend William D. Hedgespeth; friend, brother and co-laborer Reverend Brian Reed; and last, but not least, my beautiful and spirit-led aunt Vera L. Hailey-Smith. All of their efforts helped to make this book complete, and I couldn't have done it without them.

Special thanks go out to my alma mater, Paine College. There were many things that happened to me while I was there. However, the most important things were that I gained another family that spreads throughout these United States, and, that is where I met my wife! To my fraternity, Kappa Alpha Psi Fraternity, Inc. Thank you for letting me in the brotherhood. Thank you to the Epsilon Psi chapter, in particular, the "14 Kontroversial Decisions."

Lastly, to every young person I've ever talked to, while I was teaching in school, at church, or wherever we came in contact with each other, thank you, as well. You listened to me, shared your feelings, with me, cried to me, and even laughed with me. I'm grateful to God for you and hope you will find this book useful! You offered great insight on how the construction and framework of this book was to be formed. God Bless you all!!!

God Can Use You, Too!

By

A. X. Hailey

Chapter 1

God Can Use You, Too!

"Don't let anyone look down on you because you are young, but set an example for the believers in speech, in life, in love, in faith and in purity."

1 Timothy 4:12

One thing I quickly realized while I was growing up is that many people put a premium on age! It is one of those things that parents instill in their children at an early age. Sometimes you have a question about life and life's issues. As we grow older and begin to notice little nuances of life, it prompts us to ask questions about things that we don't understand. All of a sudden you are smacked with the response from your parents, "Wait until you get older" or "You're not old enough to understand." Dumbfounded, I asked myself, why do I have to wait until then? As I've gotten older, I now understand what they were saying. I've found out that if they tried to explain those things, it would not have registered. Much was beyond my understanding, and furthermore, my thirst for understanding would not have been quenched because it would have left more questions than answers.

Many of my curiosities were natural and healthy; however, the responses left me wondering: since I am young, will I ever understand? Will I get the answers I need to further my growth? Is it possible for me to make a difference in people's lives? If you, too, are asking these questions, the answer is that you can be influential while you are young. It is possible for you to make a difference. You can make an impact. Most importantly, God can certainly use you!

Young people have many things that distract them from doing things God's way. Young people want to be considered "*cool*" amongst their friends and can end up doing things that they were not taught or should not be doing at all! For example, when I was growing up, I used a lot of profanity around my friends. Now, I know that it was wrong to use such language, but I wanted to be accepted by my friends, so I talked the way they talked. I also skipped school during my middle school years. Since my friends didn't want to go to school, I decided that I didn't want to go to school either. One year I had over 20 absences! Try to explain that to your parents! I was influenced by that which was wrong instead of influencing my friends with that which is right. As I reflect back, their influence on me was much greater than I thought. Moreover, young people today are influenced not only by their friends, but by the media as well. Entertainers and athletes often seem to have more impact on their lives than their parents. Many young men are influenced by so called *"thugs."* They have replaced a genuine smile with a hard scowl. Young ladies are influenced by make-up commercials and images of *"top models"* to look a certain way. All of this can negatively impact decision making when young people believe that they don't stack up or are not worth their while.

There will always be outside forces, but why not allow God to influence you? Why fight against the One who has a track record? Why not trust the One who came through for others when things didn't go their way? Why, young people, why?

Well, the truth of the matter is, others have laid a foundation for us, telling us in verbal and non-verbal ways that God only uses "older" people to accomplish his will. Their view is you have to have prior experience before God can use you. I have one word for that, BALONEY! God can use whomever He chooses, when He wants, for however long. There are some things that can hinder you as a youngster; there are some things that you don't know yet. But, the truth of the matter is, God not only **can** use you, He **wants** to use you. If we look at the bible verse for this chapter, we'll find that in the book of

Timothy, he (Timothy) was being encouraged by the Apostle Paul. Let's look at what Paul was saying to Timothy. He said, *"Don't let anyone look down on you because you are young..."* Timothy was a young preacher and was placed over a flock of people (today he would have been a pastor at an early age, possibly around 35 to 38 years old, and although that may be old in your eyes, in the bible day, that's young). Allow me to break down this scripture to see what God is saying to us. *Don't let anyone...*, is a command (this is an imperative sentence which means it is a command or request) that means not to allow anyone to look down, scorn, make fun of, or think lightly of you. *Look down on...*, means to look down upon, despise, think little of, or devalue. *Youth*, means the state of youthfulness, age or time of youth. So, Paul is writing to encourage Timothy not to allow anyone to look down on him because he is young. Stop letting people push you around! That's not to say that Timothy should have lashed out and said some things he regretted. Rather, it is to say that Paul wanted him to stand firm in a loving and godly way. These things Paul told him are characteristics that apply to everyone, regardless of age. He wanted to suggest to him not to get discouraged because people may see him as this young, inexperienced man who many thought should not be in a position to lead people.

Paul was essentially saying to Timothy, you are capable of doing the job. You are capable to lead these people, although you are a young man. Young Timothy, do you know what you have? Do you know what sets you apart from others? You have strength, energy, fresh, new ideas, and you have the drive to get it done. So, don't let these folks devalue you because of your age. What you lack in experience, you make up in strength, energy, and drive.

We've all made mistakes in our lives, but we should learn from them and make ourselves better.

That's how you obtain experience ... by making mistakes!

Paul goes on to say, "... *but set an example for the believers in speech, in life, in love, in faith and in purity.*" In other words, let the people see that you can and will speak with intelligence. Your speech is not vulgar, but respectful. Your speech is not offensive, but encouraging. Your speech is not profanity-laced, but courteous. It's okay to say "yes ma'am" and "yes sir." Not only that, but you can allow people to see that you will live a life that is positive.

Young men, you don't have to be angry at the world. You can go to school and make something of yourselves. You can be productive citizens in this country. You can be good men to the women in your life (mother, grandmother, sister, aunt, cousin, and girlfriend). You don't have to spend time in jail for doing petty crimes. You can be good husbands and family men (which we desperately need). You can do those things.

Young ladies, you don't have to be *"trashy."* You don't have to settle for living on welfare your whole life *(welfare is and should be used to assist you in your time of need, not as your means of support, forever!*

According to Wikipedia:

The US Census declared that in 2010, 15.1% of the general population lived in poverty:

- *9.9% of all non-Hispanic white persons*
- *12.1% of all Asian persons*
- *26.6% of all Hispanic persons [of any race]*
- *27.4% of all black persons. About half of those living in poverty are non-Hispanic white (19.6 million in 2010), but poverty rates are much higher for blacks and Hispanics. Non-Hispanic white children comprised 57% of all poor rural children).*

You don't have to be two, three or four men's *"baby mamas."* You can be productive citizens of this country. You can be good wives and raise a family. You, too, can go to school and make something of yourselves. Listen! Stop letting people tell you that you are worthless! Drugs are not your friend! Alcohol isn't cool to consume, underaged! These are devices the devil uses to destroy you before you become aware of your true value!

You can be an example to everyone in your speech and in the way you live. You see, God gave Moses the Ten Commandments, and I believe that all of them are important, but the most important commandments to me are: "Love thy God" and "Love thy neighbor." Look at what it says in Matthew 22:37-40: *"Jesus said, 'Love the Lord your God with all your passion and prayer and intelligence.' This is the most important, the first on any list. But there is a second to set alongside it: 'Love others as well as you love yourself." These two commands are pegs; everything in*

God's Law and the Prophets hangs from them."
(Message Bible) The other 8 commandments will fall
into place if we love with an agape love (an
unconditional love). Paul was telling Timothy to be
an example in love. Love people and treat them
right! Love your family and do right by them! Love
yourself and don't do anything that will cause your
mind and body harm. Love yourself and don't
entertain anything that could damage your spirit
(music, images, relationships, etc.) Love, love, love! I
heard the songwriter say, *"What the world needs now,
is love, sweet love. It's the only thing that we have too
little of."* If we can show the world that, yes, I am
young, but I can love God, myself, and people, this
will be a better place. Paul encouraged Timothy to be
an example in love and in faith. Showing your faith
in God is not an *"old person's thing."* It should be an
"every person's thing." If you can show your friends
and family your availability to God, then others will
see that and be encouraged.

You can show people that you are somebody. You can demonstrate to people that you are offering yourself to God and that you are available to be used. Don't get it *"twisted"*; it can be a scary thing to follow God. You don't know where He will lead you, and furthermore, you may not want to go the way He wants you to go. I'm not trying to make it sound easy because it's not. I will tell you that there is a great benefit in serving God while you are young. There are people of all ages who need to see the younger generation doing something positive. Not just one, two, or a few of you, but a whole lot. Being young is a beautiful thing. It is the time when you are carefree about the worries of adult life. It is the time where you play games, play with toys, and yes, say the "darndest" things! However, being young doesn't mean you are worthless until you get older. God can use you now!

If you are a person whose parents take you to church and you hear some bible events talked about, let me share something with you. In the scripture used for this chapter, God used a 35 to 38 year old man (Timothy) to lead people spiritually. Remember, they were living during a time where many people lived to be a ripe old age! His age then would be the equivalent to a 15 to 18 year old. And to be frank with you, 35 to 38 years old is still relatively young by today's standards!

In the Old Testament, there were three Hebrew boys who were thrown into the fiery furnace because they refused to follow King Nebuchadnezzar's decree. They showed everyone then and now that their *faith* in God was more important than anything else. They would not cross that line of demarcation. Their faith would not allow them to bow down to anyone other than the Almighty God. It didn't matter to them that everyone else was complying or that they would be severely punished because of their refusal to obey King Nebuchadnezzar. What did matter was that they put their trust and faith in God.

They took a principled stance; they would not worship another deity other than God. This is what they said, "*If our God is able to save us, he will; even if he should not, we will not worship.*" Look at what happened. The king had his servants turn up the furnace seven times hotter than usual and threw them in. The furnace was used to bake clay pots, jars and bricks. The heat from the furnace gave the product integrity; the heat made it stronger. So they turned up the heat higher. Consequently, God didn't deliver them from the furnace; he delivered them from the *fire* while they were *in* the furnace. By the next morning they were still alive with an angel with them to protect them, and they didn't smell like smoke when they came out! Their allegiance was so strong and so evident that the king made a new decree; no one could utter an insult about the God of these three boys. If they did, they would be destroyed. Their actions made a difference in a life and possible other lives that didn't know the true and living God. Oh, and by the way, did I mention that they were youths?

There was a guy by the name of David. I'm sure you've heard of him. If not, he is the one who conquered that giant dude called, *"Goliath."* All in all, David defeated the giant with a smooth stone (he picked up five but only used one). Oh, and by the way, did I mention that he also was a youth in his late teens to early twenties?

Well, if those biblical accounts don't do anything for you, let's use someone more contemporary. Dr. Martin Luther King, Jr., is celebrated throughout this country for his bravery and the courage to stand up to injustices during the Civil Rights Era. He was arguably the leader of the entire African American race. We all know the things he did and how he did them. But do we know how old he was when he did them? Just remember, he died at the young age of 39! He was 26 years old when he led the Montgomery Bus Boycott. He was 29 years old when he led the march to Washington, D.C. He was 34 years old when he wrote and recited the now famous "I Have A Dream" speech in Washington, D. C. He was 36 years old when he led a freedom march in Selma, Alabama. Even though you may be saying that he was an older man, Dr. King got started early when he enrolled into Morehouse College at the age of 15 and received a Sociology degree at the age of 19.

So my point to you is that God can do great things with young people if you allow yourself to be used by Him. We pray and ask for certain things from God, but can He use you? Will you step up and be an example in speech, in life, in love, in faith and in purity? Just know that God Can Use You, Too!!!

Picking Your Brain: *You know I want to do what God says, but there are so many other influences around me, what should I do?*

Well, many people have different influences around them. I don't know what type of people you hang around or what influences you have, but I know there are people who can help you with your situation. I would say to surround yourself with different influences, but that's easier said than done. I have a good friend and brother (also fraternity brother in Kappa Alpha Psi, Fraternity Inc.) who has experienced some of life's ups and downs. He overcame those influences and, with the grace of God, has put himself in a position to praise God through his living. My brother and friend, Frankie Brown, has an appreciation for life and the blessings of God.

Here is his response to this question:

Dear Young Person,

Don't be influenced by people who are not Godly. We are all born with a conscience that guides us in knowing right from wrong. Then, hopefully, we learn the difference. When you know deep in your heart something is not right, don't do it. Make good choices daily, and good things will follow. The bible says in Isaiah 40:8 that "the grass withers and the flowers fall away but the word of our GOD endures forever." So everything that is not rooted in the word of GOD will not last. The guy in class who is the class clown seems cool now, but when it's time to go to college, he will have to pay while the individual who studies and listens in class will be the one who has a better chance of getting a free college education. Learn from the mistakes of others as well as their accomplishments.

Life is about sowing and reaping in all areas. The farmer sows seed to get a harvest of fruit and vegetables to bring to market and make a living. One of the ways we sow is through our choices. The choices that we make daily directly influence the quality of life we live tomorrow. If you misbehave in class today, you may end up in detention tomorrow. If you talk in class today instead of listening to the teacher, you may not pass the quiz tomorrow. Think of sowing and reaping in every area of your life and realize everything that you want in the future comes as a direct result of your actions today. The guy who starts smoking or drinking alcohol in high school may likely be the same guy who is homeless and an alcoholic by the time he is an adult while the guy who takes school and his relationship with GOD seriously is a successful businessman, pastor, teacher, lawyer, doctor, policeman, fireman etc... You are literally shaping your life with the choices you make daily, so be influenced by people who are where you want to be 20 years from now. Think of good choices as the building blocks to a successful life.

Chapter 2

Why Do They Act Like That?

2Kings 4:5, *"Now Naaman was commander of the army of the king of Aram. He was a great man in the sight of his master and highly regarded, because through him the Lord had given victory to Aram. He was a valiant soldier, but he had leprosy."*

New International Version

Church folks can be some funny people! Not just funny as in hilarious, but also funny as in peculiar. I have a long standing belief ... that traditionalism can kill a particular body within the church. What I want you to notice is that I didn't say "traditions," but I said "traditionalism." Traditions are good, traditions are fun, and traditions can bring people closer together. There is nothing wrong with traditions within the church or any other entity. The problem is "traditionalism" within the church. Here is the difference: the Merriam-Webster's Collegiate Dictionary 11th Ed. defines traditions as *an inherited, established, or customary pattern of thought, action, or behavior.* The same dictionary defines traditionalism as an *exaggeration of customs, actions, or beliefs.* There are so many traditions in the church that are wonderful. Traditionalism is one thing that can be used to put a wedge between conservative Christians and contemporary Christians. Communion or Lord's Supper is a wonderful ordinance and tradition to remember and commemorate the death, burial and resurrection of our Lord and Savior Jesus Christ. However, traditionalism takes it to a whole different level. For example, while growing up in my home church we used to have communion or the Lord's Supper at six o'clock on the first Sunday evening of every month. When I got older, I asked "Why do we have to go back to church just to have the Communion?" The response I got was because it is called the Lord's "Supper" and you have "supper" in the evening and not the morning. Having Communion in the evening because we call it the Lord's "Supper" is traditionalism. You can have it at anytime you want, but to use the explanation that you do it because it's called the "Lord's Supper" is taking it to another level. Covering up the dishes of communion with a white sheet because "we've always done it that way" is traditionalism. Some things are not necessary for us to do.

Another example is getting "dapper" to attend church services. There is a large group of people that believe that your best clothes should be worn for church. There is nothing wrong with that in and of itself, but some people take it to the extreme. While growing up, a number of people wore flashy suits and outfits to church. I took it that they were wearing those clothes to be *seen,* to have the attention on them. Being *seen* in church is the wrong motivation for going. Our motivation for attending church services should be to hear the preached Word and experience the love, encouragement and friendship of other believers. What we are wearing should be so far down on the list of things, that it really shouldn't matter. At the same time, we can't come to church any kind of way either. The point is the emphasis should not be on the clothing. Again, there is nothing wrong with those things in and of themselves because that is what people want to do, and I'm not here to mock it or say that it is wrong. That's the way some people want or like it to be. I'm not trying to pastor anyone's church. I'm not trying to move in and change how any church should run their particular services. Still, my aim is to enlighten those who wonder why young people are not attracted to the church setting.

Most church services are not set-up with young people in mind! Others have shown that keeping up with the times is important. They show this by gearing their services towards praise teams that feature songs that are more modern or up-to-date.

Young people can actually participate in the worship service. A good number of ministries are teaching subjects that people can relate to as opposed to purchasing books that have subjects that are recycled year after year. A large amount of churches have youth pastors to assist the senior pastor in dealing with everyday issues for the youth. It seems as if young people are required to conform as to how they think, act, dress and behave in order to be a part of the worship experience. Is that fair? I can't say that it is.

We want youth to attend, but we wonder why there is not a commitment to the church, Sunday School or Bible Study. There is not enough relatable programming. I am of the belief that some churches really don't know how to reach the young people in their congregations. Therefore, instead of making it seem like they are catering to one group, they continue to do what they know. That may be a harsh statement to make, but look at it from a young person's perspective. There are people in the church that act like they have been "holier-than-thou" ever since they were born. They act like they haven't done much wrong in their lives and think that quoting scripture is the answer. Explaining how that scripture can be applied should go along with that. Is that too much to ask? If you are reading this and you are a person who fits this category, my question to you is, why do you act that way? Why are you faking like you are or have been all that? Why are you acting hypocritical? A hypocrite in Greek simply means a "play-actor" or someone who is putting on a face that is not theirs. For example, you remember back in chapter one when I told you that I used to "cuss" all the time around my friends. That was me being a hypocrite. People who act like that are people who put on a *"front"* as if they are cool, but they are not. They are just ordinary people. That's what is meant by hypocrites in the church, and sadly to say, we have too many of them.

What is not realized or even admitted by many is that we all have things in our "closets" that we don't want people to know. My pastor, Rev. Jake Gaines, Jr., often says, "If everyone knew everything about everybody, then nobody would like anybody!" True statement because if your past can't serve as an example to some young person or any person, then you are not much help to them or anybody! **NEWSFLASH:** Christianity is not about us! It is not about how much you have, how much "religion" you have obtained, or how many scriptures you can quote at the drop of a hat. It's about helping somebody come closer to Christ, especially some young person!

2 Kings chapter 5 verse 1 says, *"Now Naaman was commander of the army of the king of Aram. He was a great man in the sight of his master and highly regarded, because through him the Lord had given victory to Aram. He was a valiant soldier, but he had leprosy." (NIV)* What does this have to do with church

folks? I'm glad you asked. This is the way I looked at this scripture: This was a man who was highly regarded in his community. He was like a lot of people today; he got a lot of respect from the people who were under him because of what he achieved. Naaman got along with everybody in his neighborhood. He picked up the trash on his lawn, gave the kids good advice, listened to his parents and achieved great things in his life. He went on to college and received his Bachelors Degree and then went on to the military. He worked his way up the ranks and became a commander of the army; however, it goes on to say *"but he had leprosy."* Good things can be said about everyone. We all can list the good things we have achieved: awards, scholarships, community contributions, etc. There are people who can speak highly of us, praising us for having good character.   Regardless of what we can say about ourselves, we all have a *"but"* in our character. Each one of us has some things in our lives about which we are not proud.

Adults, there are people who need to hear that you *used* to be something. They need to hear that you were at ease in wearing your skirt around your thighs. You should share with someone that you used to smoke weed all the time. The truth needs to be told about your drinking "binges" with your friends. The '80s rap group *Whoudini* had a song call "The Freaks Come Out at Night."   That was somebody's "national anthem" during their day. If we want to be "real" and honest, these experiences need to be shared because young people's views of adults are that they have never done anything on the "sneak tip." They need to hear that *you* weren't all that either, but God still loves you, and he forgave (is forgiving) you for the sins that you have committed. It's time for church folks to stop acting. It's time for church folks to realize that it is that type of attitude that can be a detriment to the growth of the Kingdom of God.

Young people need someone to be real with them and let them know that their walk or growth in Christ is not unique. We've all been through downs and taken the wrong paths. Although I accepted the Lord into my life at the age of eight, my dad had been a deacon in the church for as long as I can remember, and I've been in church all my life, I still acted foolishly once I was able to be out on my own. When I began to change the way I thought about church and wanted to become closer to God, I thought the things I was doing or did would hinder my relationship with God forever. In other words, I didn't think He would accept me back into His fellowship. I didn't grow up with people in church who were "real" with me. I wasn't around adults who explained to me that they had to "grow up" spiritually. They've always acted like they had it together. To be honest with you, once I found out that they weren't like that, it changed my opinion about them. I saw them as people who weren't being real, "were" play-acting or being "hypocritical" as opposed to those who was genuine.

When God put people in my life who were willing to share their experiences with me and showed me that God still loves me in spite of me, they were the people who I wanted to stay around. I found encouragement through *their* experiences. That's all I'm saying! Young people need someone to be "real" with them, not to put on a "front" or an act! They need a person who has been out in the world, who understands that thinking the way the world thinks will not allow you to be successful in your Christian walk. They need a person to explain that their growth in Christ is a process.

Picking Your Brain: *Why do Christians have two lives: an outside of church life where they're not acting* *like a Christian and a "praise the Lord" life when they*

get in church?

Well, there are many reasons for this. Who knows why people do the things they do. We know that ultimately, God is the judge of us all and He holds our fate in His hands. A lot of people do not realize that Christianity is not about them or their status. In fact, it is the opposite! Jesus did not come to be served, but He came **to** serve! If Jesus can come down from heaven to be a servant to others, then why can't we? I've asked a very good friend of mine to address this question. He had many different experiences in his life where he can lend his knowledge to young people in hopes that they have a clearer view to what is required of them as Christians. He has been in the ministry since he was 9 years old. My friend, Minister Brian Reed has helped many people, from preaching the Gospel, to just talking to folks who are not on the straight path, to "church folks" who think that they are "all that."

Here is his response to this question:

Dear Young Person,

*Let me attempt to answer the question, "Why do Christians have two lives?" You have an "outside of church" life where you are not acting as a Christian, and you have a "praise the Lord" life when you get in church! Well, the answer is this: That's how we've been taught! It seems that all we have seen are hypocrites! They look good on Sunday, but as soon as Sunday is over, who they really are comes out. The truth is "who they are pretending to be" is a **Christian**. But I will say this: the answer is inside of you! Stop looking at what's not, and look to the Word and find out what it says for YOU to do! The day is over for letting others be the reason why you are not who you are!*

Chapter 3

Drop It Like Its Hot!

"Therefore, since we are surrounded by such a great cloud of witnesses, let us throw off everything that hinders and the sin that so easily entangles, and let us run with perseverance the race marked out for us."

Hebrews 12:1

I've said it before. Your relationship with God "right now" is important. Neither you nor I know how much longer we have on the topside of this earth. Whether you are 13, 23, or 33, you need to have a relationship now! There are many lives being lost on a daily basis, and not all of them are older people. There are a lot of grave yards with bones that used to be young people's. Thus, this may be our last time to see our loved ones, smell fresh air, live life to the fullest, we just don't know. God is the one who takes care of us and provides for us the things that we need. What's more important than a God who takes care of His children? One of the problems our young people have is that they don't see the benefits of a relationship with God. God wants you now! Just like "Uncle Sam" wants you in the military while you are young and strong, God wants you in His army while you are young and strong, as well. What's wrong with serving God while you are young? Why do we have to wait until we are older to follow God? You know the biggest misconception out there is this: you have to have yourself together before you come to the Lord. I've heard many say they need to stop this or that, the cussing, the late partying, the fornicating, the heavy drinking, etc., before the Lord can have their life. Well, if you could have done it all yourself, then you would have done it already! Here's what I say to those who have not committed to the Lord: Whether it's you or someone you know, take all those excuses, all those reasons, all those hang-ups, and "Drop it like it's hot"!

There are many people in your life who have experienced the Lord. There are many people in your life that can tell you the benefits of having a close relationship with Him right now. There were situations in your loved ones' lives where if the Lord hadn't stepped in, it would have been "doom and gloom." Don't you think if it's good enough for your grandmother, mother, close family and friends, that it is good enough for you, too? In Hebrews chapter 12 verse 1, it says that (I'm paraphrasing) since we are (present tense) surrounded by people who have experiences, lost out on opportunities and messed up, let us throw off everything that holds us back. Let us drop those things that are keeping us from having a relationship with God, like it is hot! It goes on to also say about the sin that so easily entangles us. Sin that entangles us is not only what we do, but also how we think! Our thoughts can trip us up and keep us from effectively running a race that has been set or marked out for us. Our thoughts lead to our words, our words lead to our actions, and our actions can lead to a particular behavior, but it all starts with our thoughts.

If you don't have a church home, get one very soon. Why do you need to have one? I'm glad you asked. We watch the news reports, read the newspaper, and hear stories about teenagers who have been shot and/or killed over nonsense. We have heard about young people sexually assaulted, dying in car accidents, overdosing on drugs, and kidnapped by people who want to kill them. A church home will not prevent that from happening. Having a church home and learning what God requires from us keeps our final destination from being with the devil and his angels. When are you going to wake up and realize that the devil wants to destroy you?

When will it register that the last thing the devil wants you to do is to have a relationship with God?

How soon are you going to understand that the things of the world are going to pass away, but God's word will stand forever? Don't you know that if you love the things of the world, that you don't love God? If you desire to do the things that worldly people do, then you don't have the love of God in you. You don't believe me, let's go to the bible. 1 John chapter 2 verses 15 through 17 says, *"Don't love the world's ways. Don't love the world's goods. Love of the world squeezes out love for the Father. Practically everything that goes on in the world—wanting your own way, wanting everything for yourself, wanting to appear important—has nothing to do with the Father. It just isolates you from him. The world and all its wanting, wanting, wanting is on the way out—but whoever does what God wants is set for eternity."* (The Message Bible)

We should not delay accepting the gift of salvation because we don't know when we are going to leave this earth. Hell is real! The devil and his angels are real! So, if it and they are real, then what makes you exempt from their attacks? And, if you don't have a relationship with God, then the devil has got you right where he wants you to be ... not in fellowship with God! No, you don't have to go to church to know and love God. You don't have to go to church to read your bible or have a relationship with God. However, look at what God said. In Hebrews 10:25 from the New Living Translation, *"And let us not neglect our meeting together, as some people do, but encourage one another, especially now that the day of his return is drawing near."* So my question to you is, what do you have to stave off attacks from the devil and his angels? Who are you going to turn to? The most logical answer is God, but if you don't have a relationship with Him, what do you want Him to do? Why should He protect those who reject Him? What are you waiting on to come to the Lord?

When Jesus died for the sins of the world, he didn't die for Christians. Jesus died for the ones who did not have a relationship with God so that we all could have a relationship with the Lord! Romans chapter 5 verse 8 says, *"But God demonstrates his own love for us in this: While we were still sinners, Christ died for us." (NIV)* We all were on our way to eternal damnation, but God saw fit to give us another chance and send His son to die for the sins of everyone. So if that is the case, then you can drop all your excuses and hang-ups and come to know who God is. What's stopping you ... your friends? Bring them with you. Is it your family? Bring them with you. Is it your boyfriend or girlfriend? Bring them with you. Have them to experience living life in the Lord with you because when tough times come, and they will, you are going to need someone who understands Godly support.

Contrary to popular belief, Christianity is not boring; it can be fun! You won't be lacking in anything. You have friends who like the same things you do in Christianity. You have a support system in Christianity. You definitely have love in Christianity. What more do you want? There are some adult Christians that live a boring life. You can go to the movies. You can hang out with friends whether they are Christians or not. You can go to parties or get-togethers, provided you do not have the same mindset as the ones engaging in "whatever." So, if the idea or notion that Christianity is boring is keeping you from growing, developing, or even having a relationship with God, then you need to drop that thought like it's hot, too!

Picking Your Brain: *I'm a teen with many dreams and aspirations. I want to get closer to God, but it*

seems like I can't stay away from the dumb stuff.
What should I do?

Doing dumb stuff is what I used to specialize in! Staying away from the "dumb stuff," as you say, is hard to do for some people. You don't have to live that way. Making the right decisions will help out with the "dumb stuff." Evaluating what you are doing before you do it will help, along with prayer and guidance from God. I have a good friend and brother who has experienced a lot and has seen a lot of things. He, too, is in education; he has a Masters Degree in teaching and has been a minster for 15 years. So, I'll let Minister William Hedgespeth answer your question.

Dear Young Person,

What we have to remember as Christians, even as young Christians, is Romans 3:23 says, "For all have sinned and come short of the glory of God." Even though we are Christians, we still struggle with sin. Does that mean that we should throw in the towel and keep sinning? No, Paul outlines his argument against continuing in sin in Romans 6:1-13. It doesn't mean that we give up in those times where we are struggling with sin. Those are the times that we need to draw closer to God. What is also important during those times is that we should confess our sins so that we can be forgiven (1st John 1:9). We must also forgive ourselves and let go of the guilt that we might have. Even Paul said when I would do good, evil is present with me (Romans 7:13-25). The key here is not to let it hang over you. Ask God for forgiveness, forgive yourself and move on. God Bless!

Chapter 4

Seize the Day!

We must quickly carry out the tasks assigned us by the one who sent us. The night is coming, and then no one can work.

John 9:4 (NLT)

This chapter is not about working, per se, but it is about looking within yourself and deciding what it is you want to do with your life.   There are many opportunities for you to go further educationally, professionally, and spiritually.   There is an abundance of careers suitable to whatever personality you have. There are professions that could use your energy, your drive, your know-how to help someone and, quite frankly, put a little money in your pocket. So, if that is the case, why are there so many people who don't want to do better? We must go out and seize the opportunities placed before us.   We live in a society where everything is instant, where we want things right now, at a moment's notice. Televisions have remote controls. We can change the channel instantly, but in earlier years we had to actually get up and go to the television to manually change the channel. We have microwavable meals where in a matter of minutes you have a meal to eat (ever wondered what was done before the microwave?). We have computers to look up information as opposed to going to the library to do research. I mean almost everything is instant! But the one thing that I want you to understand is that building a career *cannot* be instant. Your growth isn't instant! It can't be "I start today and tomorrow I'm done;" it has to be built over time. There's an old saying, "Rome wasn't built in a day." That is a reference to the Roman Empire, one of the most powerful empires in our world's history that took years to build. But with you, with all of us, the leg work has to start while in school. If you are reading this and you are in middle school, please, I beg you to start taking your education seriously now! If you are in high school, stop worrying about things that are not of major, life-changing importance and start taking your education seriously. If you are in Job Corp or not in school at all, learn and develop a skill that will further you because you never know how God will use you later.

Education has always been and will always be a cornerstone in building careers and communities. Education gives you the discipline to focus on what you have to do. Education puts you in a better position to support yourself and your family. Education doesn't make you better than someone else, it just puts you in a better position than those who didn't and will not obtain a formal education. I know that you have heard this before, but it bears repeating: There were those who died for the right just to know how to read, who wanted to be educated so badly, they would risk their lives to be taught how to read and write. There were those who put their lives on the line to help someone else become literate. Even then, they understood the value in being educated. Understand that being educated and getting an education are two different things. Being educated is knowing how things and entities of society work; understanding not only things in textbooks, but also learning and staying abreast of things politically, in your local community, historically, etc. Getting an education is going to school (college or trade school) to get a job or to help start a career/business. I want you to get both!

We need young people to step up and be leaders in the future. We need our young people to take on the task of caring about being educated. I know that playing sports is important to some of our youth because it was for me. I know that the "prom" and hanging out with your friends are important. I know keeping up with the times is a major thing for you right now (Facebook, Twitter, cell phones, etc.). All those things seem important now, but in the long haul, they may not be all that substantial. So guess what? You need to seize the day. You need to take advantage of the opportunities you have now. You need to set yourself apart from others who don't want to make anything of themselves. When I was a teacher in Detroit, I came across many students who were so worried about the non-essential things that the essential things were pushed to the back burner. They skipped school on a regular basis. They joked around all the time in class. They didn't **STUDY**! They did just enough to get by. They did just enough to fool their teachers, their parents, and their loved ones. They fooled everyone into thinking they were on top of their grades, all the while cheating off someone's papers. They were taking shortcuts to receive a favorable report card. After parents review the report card and find good markings, joy and sometimes relief overwhelm them. The perception is the grade is more important than the content learned. In reality, their child *"don't know jack"*! Then, when it's time to graduate or go on to the next grade/level academically, the student comes up short and blames everything and everyone. This is a cycle that desperately needs to be broken!

How Do We Break This Cycle?

We break this cycle by seizing the opportunities while they are there.   Here, in this verse that is dedicated to this chapter, Jesus is walking along His "merry way" with His disciples when they saw a blind man. The disciples confronted Jesus with this question, *"Why was this man born blind? Was it because of his own sins or his parents' sins?" (John 9:2 NLT)* Jesus answered them, *"It was not because of his sins or his parents' sins. This happened so the power of God could be seen in him. We must quickly carry out the tasks assigned us by the one who sent us. The night is coming, and then no one can work. But while I am here in the world, I am the light of the world."* (John 9: 3-5 NLT). Jesus was saying that there was an opportunity to change an outcome of a situation. There was an opportunity to make an impact on this man's life and do something positive. What He was saying was, while there is life in His body, while there are still opportunities to take advantage of, while you have life in your body, seize the day! While you have the ability to play sports to help pay for college, seize the day! While you are flexible enough to dance to pay for college, seize the day! While you have an instrument that you can play extremely well, seize the day! While you are articulate enough to write a book, seize the day! For when night comes, no one can work. The night is no more opportunities, no more chances, no more life! Jesus goes on to say in verse 5, *"but while I am here in the world, I am the light of the world."* Jesus is a different type of light than any of us can or will ever be. But we can be lights, too! We can be positive influences on the people we love, the people who are watching us from afar, and on this society. You have to seize the opportunities by working hard, real hard, not just getting by. You will not have a lot of opportunities to take advantage of, but God can open doors that many think could never be open. But He's not going to continue opening doors for us if we are not seizing the opportunities! We have to do it and show the world that God is here working in our lives. So come on, young people, SEIZE THE DAY!

Picking Your Brain: *I'm still young and want to try some things. I feel like if I don't have fun now, then I won't be able to have any experiences to share with my kids when I get older. How can I follow God and still have my fun?*

I have a good friend who works closely with young people. He and I go way back to our college days. I knew even then that he was a child of God, but like myself, he didn't always act like it. We have done some crazy things in college, and from that, this brother has a tremendous testimony. Therefore, I urge you to listen to this brother's advice. He is Pastor Dominique Johnson, organizer of the Kingdom Life Church in Macon, GA, mentor to young men and women, and a regular blog contributor to websites www.urbanscholar.com and

www.seedsglobalblog.org.

Here is his response to the question:

Dear Young Person:

Looking at the above statements brings several things to my mind. And instead of answering the questions straight out, which I might eventually do, I would like to dialogue and maybe pose reflective questions of my own. It could be considered presumptuous to assume you will live to be older. In the book of Ecclesiastes 12:1 we are told to "remember" the Lord while we are young.

It appears that the main focus here is fun. Can one not try things now that are considered to be fun while still living a life for God? If not, then that is usually called sin and is considered to lead to death. It appears that there might need to have a mind renewal, to think that to live for God means that there is no fun involved or that those who are dedicated to the Lord in their "walk" with Him do not have fun. This is a trick of the enemy and an issue that must be addressed in some fashion by the church. Jesus said that he came that we may have life, which means the God kind of life. The experiences you share with your children can be one of a life filled with the joys of serving God with all your heart. It doesn't have to be of us dwelling on nights at the club or of us smoking and drinking and participating in behavior that is antithetical to the ways of God.

After my rededication to serving God wholeheartedly and a lifestyle of holiness, there was a group of us who got together and did fun things together. We went to the movies, played cards, board games, fellowships, studied the word together, etc. I remember it being one of the best times of my life because I knew I was in the will of God. It was good, clean fun, and I didn't have to have the hangover to go with it or the consequences of a potential guilt due to more premarital sex. So my question again is what is your idea of fun? God didn't send Jesus for us to be the "frozen chosen," but to experience life to the fullest with Him and with others. Once again, maybe you need to be "transformed by the renewing of your mind." (Rom. 12:1) Don't put off today because we really don't know what tomorrow brings. When we know better, we should do better, because we are told that those of us that know to do better and don't will have to answer to God. Don't trample over the blood of Jesus and the grace of God. Blessings!!

Chapter 5

Will The Real Young Worshippers Please Stand Up!

Be thankful in all circumstances, for this is God's will for you who belong to Christ Jesus. **1Thessalonians 5:18(NLT);** *I will praise the LORD at all times. I will constantly speak his praises.* **Psalm 34:1**

New International Version

At what point in time did we forget about God? When did it become popular to not acknowledge God in public? Was it when they took prayer out of the schools? Was it when the homosexuals in the closet began to come out in droves? Or, was it when the atheist movement began to make waves about there being no God? We have literally become a nation full of forgetful people. We have forgotten that He has delivered us in ways that are just unexplainable. The question is, why? Why have we become so forgetful about God? Why isn't there regular acknowledgement of His goodness, grace and mercy? Do you know why we were created? One reason we were created was to give an invisible God visibility. Huh? I can hear you ask that question. We can't see God, we can't physically feel God, we can't hear God, but the bible says that God created man (human beings) after His image and after His likeness. That can mean that we are the closest thing to God! We are created to think like God thinks, although not on His level because it says in Isaiah 55:9, *"For just as the heavens are higher than the earth, so my ways are higher than your ways and my thoughts higher than your thoughts."* We are supposed to represent God, we are supposed to act like we are Godly, and we are supposed to treat others like God would treat them. We don't have the authority or power that God has, but we should be a representative of God in the visible. Jesus said in John 13:35, *"Your love for one another will prove to* the world that you are my disciples." Another reason we were created is to house the Holy Spirit to worship and praise God. David says in Psalm 34:1, "I will bless the LORD at all times: his praise shall continually be in my mouth."

So why can't you praise God? You know, a lot of you are adolescents, and you just want to have fun and not worry about "grown-up" matters. You just want to go to school and hang out with your friends. You just want to get on the computer and post comments on your social networking sites. You just want to go to the movies and go to parties, or if you are old enough, go to the club. One of your main concerns is to have enough money so that you can purchase the "latest and greatest." Some of you are even planning to go to college to further yourself educationally. Well, all that is good and is not harmful to you. However, those things in and of themselves will not show what kind of worshipper you are. What does show the kind of worshipper you are is your attitude behind your actions. When a person who was created in the image and likeness of God lives life with the right attitude and spirit, God gets the glory and the praise. You don't have to be at church to praise God! As a matter of fact, our praise should be done before we even get to a church. By the time we show up (those of you who actually go), we should be publicly demonstrating the goodness God has shown us throughout the week. There are many ways we can praise God. Here are some ways that a true young worshipper can stand up.

You Can Praise God In Your Talk!

No one is with you 24 hours a day, 7 days a week but God! So only you and He know what you say all day and every day. Your discourse or your talk should be positive at all times. Understand what I'm trying to tell you. I'm not saying to be a robot and program yourself to say the right things at all the right times. And I'm not saying to walk around saying "praise the

Lord," "hallelujah" all the time, either. That's ridiculous! I am saying to be polite in your vocabulary; you don't have to use vulgar words. You might get angry and let an unsavory word loose, but every other word? Be real! That's not professional, that's not polite, and it's certainly not God-like. Say "Yes ma'am" and "Yes sir" to your elders, it's okay. Speak properly when you are in a formal setting. Try not to criticize people publicly. Pull them aside and tell them what you feel in a private setting instead of embarrassing them in front of others. Now these things may sound lame and/or unpopular, but they are necessary in your everyday worship. While you are doing this, God is getting the glory. Then people will see that there is something about that young man or young lady that is different from the other young people. They will speak highly of you and all the while you are giving God glory because you are doing what He wants you to do!

You Can Praise God In Your Actions!

Being a young person in this day and time can be hard to do. I know because I was your age one time not too long ago. Times were difficult for me, and times are sometimes difficult for you! That should not be overlooked at any point. If God blesses you to have children and see them grow up, you will see some facets that are difficult to understand. You may ask yourself why their behaviors and trends are acceptable common practices. There are so many places where you can get an abundance of information. You can see people's views on all sorts of things, but when it comes down to Christianity, religion, or moral living, the views will run the gamut! I mean people will say that you can do what you want to do, when you want to do it and however you want to do it as long as you don't hurt anyone! Or, you may hear, "religion is for idiots because God isn't real!" Another thought that may come up is, if there is a God then why so much death, corruption and negativity? There are people who say these things. Unfortunately, there are some Christians who are agreeing with these comments by their actions. We, as Christians, have given the world a reason to look at us no differently than them because our actions are no different than theirs! We have sex before marriage when God said that it was only meant for husband and wife. We use profanity *relentlessly* like them when we are supposed to be the ones who can say it a different way. We live with boyfriends and girlfriends when God said that He ordains marriage, not living together! We party hard! We shouldn't partake of these things! You can live your life, and you can have fun living your life, but it is how we are to live our lives that makes us different from everyone else. You will get talked about, you will get criticized, and you will be ridiculed, but God wants some true young worshippers to show people how to live a fulfilling life at a young age!

You Can Praise God With Your Attitude!

Your discourse and your actions will be complemented with the right attitude! Your attitude is your personal view or feeling about something. How do you personally feel about the things that are done by people? Are you approving of the actions and behaviors of people around you, or are you disapproving of them? As young people, your thoughts on matters can be influenced by your parent(s), guardian(s), loved ones, mentors, etc. Prayerfully, those people are teaching you right. I am of the belief that life is partially what happens to us but mainly how we react to it. There's a saying: *when life gives you lemons, make lemonade!* That means whatever situation you are in, make the best of it. Don't walk around with your head down; instead, find something positive in the situation. You never know, someone may be watching to see how you handle certain situations, and your attitude can be an inspiration to others.

I want to encourage you to count your blessings. We all have trials (tests) that we go through. We all have situations that will weigh heavily on our minds. We can moan, groan and complain about our plight in life. Or, we can count our blessings that we are still alive with our mental and physical faculties well functioning. A long-drawn-out negative attitude will make you dejected, whereas a positive attitude with prayer will get the wheels churning on finding a solution to the problem. God will not do anything for us that we can do ourselves! So if you are prayerful, ask God to help you in making the right decisions. He'll direct you in the right direction.

When you are dealing with people, there has to be the understanding that no one can change the way people will act. The thing that we have that can set us apart is our attitude. People can be cruel! Their words towards you can be hurtful. They will taunt you or discriminate against you. Does worrying over what was said or done to you make you any happier? No. In 1995, there was a movie named *Friday*, directed by F. Gary Gray, performed by Ice Cube, Chris Tucker, and Nia Long. One of the characters in the movie was a guy named, Deebo. He was a big, muscular and mean guy. If he wanted someone's chain, then he took it. If he wanted some money, he took it. In one scene, a guy came to ask for the bike that Deebo "borrowed" and got punched in the eye (too funny)! Everyone was scared of Deebo, but at the same time, everyone was tired of Deebo pushing them around. Finally, at the end of the movie, Ice Cube's character, "Craig," dealt with Deebo the only way he knew how. Craig used fisticuffs to deal with Deebo. From that movie, I've always identified people like Deebo as Deebos. Deebos are bullies.

There have always been young people "deeboeing" other young people. They use not only physical force, but also words, messages or pictures on Facebook, Twitter, or other social media to degrade, discriminate, ridicule, or mock. A lot of young people have experienced depression and low self-esteem. Some have even resorted to suicide. I talked about growing up because of my skin complexion. It seemed like everyone had a negative comment when the subject of me and my complexion came up. I heard it from everywhere and everyone (so it seemed). I began to develop low self-esteem and didn't like the way I looked. I would get upset and often wanted to fight whenever someone said something about me. I haven't always been the biggest guy in the world, and I wasn't Craig from the movie, so I felt that my attitude should change. Instead of getting upset over what was said, I began to laugh with them which took away the sting of being hurt. And since they saw they could no longer hurt me with that, it eventually stopped.

Now let me say that this strategy may not work in all situations, but I will say that when you change your attitude towards whatever it is you are dealing with, God will step in and help you in your time of need. He wants to see what kind of attitude you have. Your attitude can give you and someone else hope and strength and can bring about a healing. When people see you, they should wonder what's behind your "swag." That's when you can tell them that it is the *God* in you that allows you to have the "swag" you have.

You can praise Him *now*! Praising Him in your talk, in your actions and in your attitude will help in your Christian walk. I didn't say it was going to be easy or without challenges, but you can do it! Philippians 4:13 says, *"For I can do everything through Christ, who gives me strength."* That simply means we can accomplish our goals and overcome our fears through the help of Jesus Christ. So, I'll say to you again, will my real young praisers please stand up!!!

Picking Your Brain: *I like to praise God, but I don't know how. What should I do? How should I act? I'm*

afraid my friends may laugh at me for wanting to do
the right thing. I need some advice.

Your friends should respect your feelings toward things. However, knowing what I know now about young people, your friends may not be mature enough to handle you wanting to praise God in your living. Let's be real, most people think that praising God is left for church on Sunday. Well, I have someone close to me who can articulate it a little better than I can. This person is my Aunt Vera Hailey-Smith. She is an active member of her church in Cincinnati, OH. She serves as a trustee and works closely with the youth department. Professionally, she works as an accountant. Let's see what she has to say to your question.

___

Dear Young Person,

Praising God ... There is no right or wrong way to
praise God. God is always pleased whenever we honor

and praise Him as long as we do it in spirit and in truth ... and with a humble and sincere heart. What I do know and understand about God is that without him I am non-existent. So, I owe my very existence to him. How can I not praise God for that alone? But wait a minute! He is so much more to me. Because of His power, I am convinced ... He is all powerful, and with him I can do all things. How can I not praise God for that? He is my protector ... praise God ... He is my redeemer ... praise God ... He is my shelter in the storm ... praise God ... He is King of Kings ... praise God ... He is my everything ... Oh, praise God. When you think of all that God is to you and what he has done for you, it is so very easy to worship and praise Him.

When I acknowledge God for all that He is to me by giving him my highest praise and worship, that's when I feel closest to the Lord. And when I am closest to God ... I feel his power in me ... the power to overcome and to be a blessing to someone else. I feel the power to be all that God desires of me ... the power to be a conqueror. There is no better feeling for me than to be in the presence of God, and with that power, what others may think no longer matters. There is a confidence in knowing and praising God!

Amen!

Chapter 6

You Are Not Alone!

"Don't be obsessed with getting more material things. Be relaxed with what you have. Since God assured us, "I'll never let you down, never walk off and leave you," we can boldly quote, God is there, ready to help; I'm fearless no matter what. Who or what can get to me?" **Hebrews 13:5-6**

Message Bible

I have to admit, I admire people who have gone through life altering situations and have overcome them. I've heard of people who have gone through circumstances ranging from rape to murder. A lot of those occurrences were beyond their control. They didn't know how to handle them or didn't know whom to turn to. I can only imagine the events that took place, from beginning to end (if there is an end), that have permanently left scars on their emotions. There may be someone reading this that is going through issues: a parental divorce, rape, incestuous relationship, pregnancy or homosexuality. I want you to know that you are not alone in your struggle to overcome these things! There are people who have gone through these, and more, who are a part of the family of God. If you are committed to God and His commandments, then you will get the benefits of His love. If you ask Him to help you, He will send someone in your life that can help you overcome your issues. It doesn't necessarily have to be a believer either! That is one of the beauties of God and His nature. He can use anyone, at anytime, with anything or any condition, in any situation, to help anybody! That's why I can tell you at this time that you are not alone. I heard this analogy from someone, and I'll use it for this point. There are many stairs on an escalator. An escalator moves to another level where a person wants to go, whether it is going up or going down. You can stomp on the stairs of the escalator, you can spit on the stairs of the escalator, or you can write on and scratch up the stairs of the escalator. Whatever you do to it, those stairs are still going to carry you and take you to whatever level you want to go. I said that to mean, God uses us to help take each other to another level. There are people who have been raped, gone through the hurt and pain of a parental divorce, committed crimes, gotten pregnant at an early age, are homosexual or have overcome their feelings of homosexuality. Whatever their situation is or was, they have gotten "beaten up" (mentally, physically, emotionally, and/or spiritually) about it. But, God can still use them to help someone else in their situation and help take them to another level. He's not going to operate like He did in the bible days. You know why? He doesn't have to! He has us to be an encouragement to each other, to uplift spirits, to listen to, to give a loving hug when it is needed or a pop upside the head. He has us to criticize our actions when we do something wrong!

Don't get it "twisted"! God does not like some of the actions we take. God does not like some of our behaviors. I hear so often from people that "God loves me," He loves everyone! Guess what, God loves the murderer, the drug abuser, the drunk, the prostitute, the pimp, the drug dealer, but He HATES the activity. God HATES sin! You heard about the event with our Lord and Savior Jesus Christ. You heard about what He did on the cross, right? Well, let's look at that event. It states in the gospels that Jesus was on the cross from the 6th to the 9th hour (from 12:00 noon to 3:00 in the afternoon). While He was on the cross, it is stated that the sun refused to shine. In that instance, that was when God was turning away from Jesus because He looked at Jesus and saw nothing but every sin that was ever committed and every sin that will be committed by everyone. So, if God can't look at His begotten Son with sin on His shoulders, then what makes anyone think that God can look at us with *our* sin on *our* shoulders? The only way God can look at us is through the blood of Jesus. Because of that event, we are now able to have a relationship with God.

If you are living in sin, then I encourage you to repent and turn away from that. Repenting means to ask for forgiveness and not to do it anymore. If the sun did not shine in mid-day when Jesus was on the cross, then just imagine if God was to turn away from us; how much darkness would consume or engulf our lives? I'm not talking about it being cloudy. I'm talking the sun not shining at all and complete darkness. We need the Lord in tough times. We need the Lord in good times. You are not in this fight alone! God is with you, so when are you going to call on Him? When are you going to put ALL your trust in Him?

That reminds me of a song by Jennifer Hudson. Yea, the same Jennifer Hudson who was on American Idol (jokingly called American Karaoke) and the hit movie, *Dream Girls*. Well, she performed a song entitled "Spotlight." She talks about her man keeping a close eye on her because she thinks he might be afraid of her going to find someone else to take his place in her life. The chorus of the song goes: *Well, I don't like living under your spotlight, just because you think I might find somebody worthy. Well, I don't like living under your spotlight. Baby, if you treat me right, you won't have to worry.* Well, I want you to know that God does like living under *your* spotlight because you won't find another more worthy than Him! He wants you to always be watching, always looking to Him. He wants us to always trust and depend on Him. It does not matter the circumstances or the situations, God is there to help you in your time of need. You may not think He is there. You may not even feel or see His presence, but that's why He has others and me who love you, to encourage you along your walk. So, no, you are not alone! God is always ever present! Therefore, say with confidence, *The LORD is my helper, so I will have no fear.*

Picking Your Brain: *It seems like when I go to adults to talk to them about my problems at home, school, or whatever, the only thing they tell me to do is pray. I have prayed a lot, but things keep happening to me. I want someone to help me and encourage me because sometimes I feel like giving up.* Well, giving up without exhausting all your options that are available to you is not good. We have to keep in mind that things will happen to us while we live this life. It's how we respond to those things that will make us stronger and enable us to get through them. Like I said before, everyone has some rough spots in their life. God didn't always have them go through them because they did something wrong! He used them in the event that someone, maybe you, would look to them in time of need. My college friend, Candace Greene, has gone through some things in her life where she can help someone along the way. She is a wife, mother, entrepreneur (Cherishedflight Communications, LLC. Check her out on Facebook), and most importantly, a lover of God, who lives in Baltimore, Maryland.

Here's her response to the question:

Dear Young Person,

I do agree with the other adults when they tell you to pray because prayer is a lifeline between you and God. What they failed to tell you is that prayer does not have to be a big production, but a simple conversation you have with the Lord. All you have to do is start talking to God, and he will listen to you. BUT, also understand that your time with Him is a two-way street. Don't think you're going to get to do all of the talking! You also must listen for Him to respond. What you will learn is that God has a sense of humor and will answer you in very interesting and unique ways. Sometimes his response will come in the form of a song, on a license plate or billboard. You may hear your answer in a snippit of someone else's conversation, a television commercial, or in spoken words between characters in a movie. All you have to do is be open to communicating with God. You're never too young to get this dialogue going. Try it. You may find you'll become hooked!

Chapter 7

Memo to the Parents

I have spoken throughout this book to the young people and young adults, but now I want to turn my attention to the parents and those of you who desire to be parents or are about to be a parent. First let me tell you that I am a parent of two wonderful girls. My daughters are the joy of my life, and as a father, I feel an awesome responsibility to raise them in a drama-free, loving, Christian household. I feel like my role in their lives is to be that figurehead that loves them and provides the discipline that they need. They need to see the way I interact with my wife, so they will know what to look for in a man when it is time for them to choose a mate. I want them to pay attention to the contact I have with my parents, so they will have an understanding of what a parent/child relationship should be now and when they get older. My daughters only have each other as siblings; therefore, my kinship with my siblings is important for them to know what is required of them as siblings to one another. That's not to say that I am the best at any of the roles I have. My prayer is always to help me be the best husband, father, son, brother, family member and friend that I can be. I ask the Lord to let me be a blessing to my pastor and church family, not a hindrance. That's why it is imperative for *us* parents to understand that what we do, what we say, and how we act (or don't act) are being filtered through the minds of our children. They are taking everything we do, say, or act into account, and some day they are going to play back those things to us at the right (depending on whom you ask) or wrong time. We set the tone for how our children grow up.

Let me step back to say that I'm not here to try and give parenting tips to anyone. I'm not here to tell you that I have the answers to any challenge our children gives us because if I can remember, no one gave us a manual book as we left the hospital with our children! This is merely to let you know, as a former educator and current minister, that I hear and see things from our youth and from some parents that are baffling. Well, having said that, let me tell you what I understand. These things you have heard before, but they bear repeating, and I believe they can be helpful.

Parents Are the First Teachers Children Have!

You didn't know that? We, as parents, teach our children just about everything they know. I say "just about" because they are influenced by other people, media, music, etc., entities parents can't compete with! We don't teach them by sitting them down and talking or lecturing to them. We teach them mainly by our actions! And, quite frankly, sometime our actions contradict what we say. It is good that we push our children to get educated or to get an education (see the difference between the two in the chapter, "Seize the Day"), but we just can't be happy with a good letter grade. We have to be concerned about their study habits, and the content they are learning and supposed to learn for their grade level (Grade Level Content Expectations). We should want to know from the teacher if they are learning the material, if they are struggling with anything, does the teacher need you as the parent to do anything on your end to make their learning better. Instead, some parents see the grades and feel assured that everything is all right. Well, here's a newsflash: an A or a B is not the only measuring stick in determining the intelligence of a child--just like a D or an F doesn't determine the ignorance of a child. There are many elements that factor in a child's education, and when the parent just looks at the grade and puts everything on that letter, then he is sending the message that the grade is more important than what they are learning. That's why we have students who don't do anything for most of the card marking, then wait until it is close to receiving their report card assessment, then try and make up work, turn in old assignments, and cheat just to get a decent/good grade!

We teach them in the spiritual realm as well. We go to church sometimes, and "praise the Lord." We get "emotional" and cry when the spirit moves us. We sing in the choir or on the praise team. We shout on moving songs or on the sermons; our children see all that. But, when we go home on Monday through Saturday, we are not the same "holy ghost- filled" people our children saw on Sunday at church. Those are mixed signals that children don't need to see. If going to church and having a relationship with God is important (and I assume that it is, otherwise you would not be reading this), then we need to let our children know that, not only in our words, but also in our actions!

When things get tough in our lives, and they will, we can't turn our backs on God and begin to do things our way. We can't stop going to church! We can't stop praising God because our marriage is going bad. Worship is in order even if we lost our job. God still loves us even when we are disobedient to him, so our love shouldn't stop because we disagree with our Christian brother or sister. My pastor (Rev. Jake Gaines, Jr., of the Synagogue Baptist Church in Detroit, MI) preached a sermon titled: "Can You Still Praise God While It Is Raining?" If you have a relationship with God, your children need to know where you stand with that. I'm not telling you not to have fun, enjoy life, or be lively. I'm just saying our children need to know that having God in our lives is much more important than going to the club or any other way we have fun! This brings me to my next point:

Parents Instill Values In Children

You didn't know this, either? I'm sure you did, and again, these are just reminders. Parents instill values in children every day of that child's life. I have seen a lot of children from all different walks of life. The one thing that stands out in children who have parents that are involved in their lives or are not involved in their lives is ... behavior! You can watch a child for 30 minutes to an hour, and you can tell (I could anyway) what type of household that child lives in. Children learn their values from their parents. Didn't you? Didn't you learn how to act around adults from your parents, that when you go to school you were there for school and not to clown around in class? Didn't you learn the value of hard work from home? Well, if "you" learned those things and more from "your" parents, who do you think your children are going to learn theirs from :Santa Claus, Sesame Street, or how about Lady GaGa? No, they are going to learn from you and me, the parents!

Even in our spiritual lives, we teach values. Give your child something they can take with them throughout their years, something that is going to sustain them when times get difficult. Instill in them that prayer changes situations by changing people's hearts and actions. I know we say "prayer changes things." However, we can pray that our couches turn to a pile of money, but when we open our eyes, that couch is still a couch! You get the point. The bible says in Proverbs 22:6, *"Train a child in the way he should go, and when he is old he will not turn from it."(NIV)* An important note about this verse: First, the book of Proverbs is a book of suggestions; it is not church doctrine. However, these are suggestions I would pay heavy attention to because it's in the bible and the wisest man who ever lived, Solomon, said it.

Solomon was "dropping some knowledge on us." We can certainly say that however we train our children, and whatever we taught them or didn't teach them will be the way they are going to be. So, we teach our children how to be mean by being mean to them and other people. We teach them that it's okay not to forgive people and to hold grudges. We illustrate how to be respectful by being respectful to *our* elders and parents in front of them. I told the young people this, and I'll tell the parents, too: it's ok to say "yes ma'am and yes sir" to the elders; that's a way we can "honor" our parents!

We teach self-respect by respecting ourselves through our grooming techniques (appearance) and our speech. Our children need to understand that society will judge them on two things initially: how they look and how they talk. If you are looking any kind of way and talking any kind of way, then guess what? It will be like I said in the beginning of this chapter: your child is taking mental notes and will play back that scene at the most inopportune time. I remember one time when my oldest daughter was about 3 years old. I saw something that was disturbing to me, at which time I blurted out, "What the hell?" Well, some time down the line when she saw something that was confusing or disturbing in her mind, guess what she said? We all want the best for our children, to excel educationally and develop into good people. However, we have to understand as parents that our job is an awesome task for anyone to do. That means we have to set good examples so our children can know what to do and how to do it, and what to say and how to say it. That doesn't mean that our mistakes are off limits to our children. You decide what you will tell your children at the right time, but they need to know that their parent(s) have made some mistakes, maybe even major ones that you have overcome with the grace of God. Our present and past struggles can be used as teaching tools for our children. I said it before. God doesn't always punish us with our problems. Sometimes He merely uses us so that we can be a witness for Him to others who have done the same things. Our children can learn from our mistakes. Wouldn't you want someone to help you and guide you while going through the pitfalls in your life? Just imagine if you could go back in time and be around yourself at the age of 16. What would you tell yourself? What would you keep yourself from doing that gave you pain and heartache later in life? Our children are that age. We need to go back and keep them from falling in the same traps we fell in. Will they listen to us? No, not all the time! In fact, it may take someone else to tell them the same things you have been telling them for a long time, but they still need to know and hear it from loving people.

Our children also need to know that God is the most important entity in our lives. Jazz musician,

Jonathan Butler, recorded a song that said, "Falling in love with Jesus was the best thing I've ever done." If that is your sentiment as well, then our children need to know that by the way we serve Him at all times. But hey, I know you knew that already ... I just wanted to remind you. God Bless!

27555381R00065

Made in the USA
Charleston, SC
14 March 2014